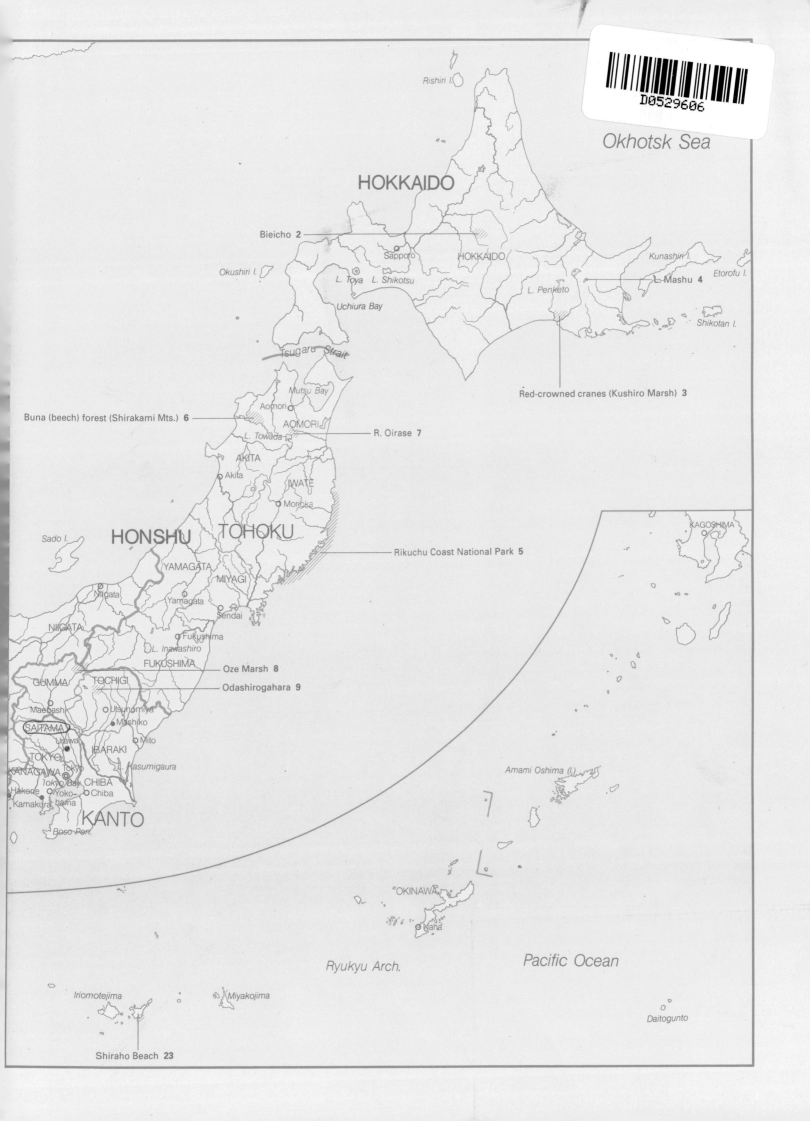

J A P A N
A Living Portrait

JAPAN

A Living Portrait

FOREWORD BY MIKE MANSFIELD

NOTE: In accordance with Japanese custom, names of Japanese people are given with the family name first, followed by the given name, except for those listed in the Photo Credits and Acknowledgments, which follow Western convention.

PHOTO CREDITS

(Roman numerals refer to chapter, arabic numerals to color plates. Pages are given for unnumbered plates.)

Yukio Amano, I: 1; Lucy Birmingham, II: 36; Bon Color Photo Agency, p. 5 (top), I: 10, 18; Brian Brake, II: 28; Camera Tokyo Service, p. 1; Color Box, p. 7 (right); Cosmo Photo Office, II: 5; Fine Photo Agency, I: 7, 19, 20; Mitsumasa Fujitsuka, IV: 7; Steve Gardner, p. 7(left), II: 7, 29, III: 9, 10, 16; Eberhard Grames, front jacket; Hideo Haga, II: 44; M. Hasegawa, II: 1; Tsuneo Hayashida, I: 3; Sadao Hibi, III: 14, 33, 35; Naotaka Hirota, III: 31; Takeshi Hosokawa, II: 51; Kazuo Ishikawa, II: 50; Yasuhiro Ishimoto, III: 32; Katsuji Iwao, II: 12; Japan Performing Arts Center, IV: 11; Japan Travel Bureau, II: 41; Yasuhiro Kashiwabara, II: 48; Hisao Kawahara, III: 7, 8; Takeshi Kawamoto, I: 14; Lab Tokyo, III: 26; Shinzo Maeda, I: 2, 4; Shohei Matsufuji, I: 16; Kazuo Matsuura, I: 17; Chuji Minematsu, III: 39; Yasuhiko Miyajima, III: 20; Katsuhiko Mizuno, II: 30; Akira Nakata, II: 35, 38; National Noh Theater, III: 5, 6; National Theater of Japan, III: 4; Nijo Castle, III: 28; Akio Nonaka, II: 42; Okinawa Koho Center, I: 23; P. Riel, II: 26; Joseph Rupp, II: 34; Tetsuro Sato, II: 25; Hans Sautter, p. 5 (bottom), II: 6, 16, 17, 19, 22, 32, 33, 43, IV: 1; Koga Sekido, III: 27; Tatsuzo Shimaoka, III: 44; Shinjuan, III: 29; Shinkenchiku-sha, IV: 8, 9; Kishin Shinoyama, III: 36; Shiro Shirahata, I: 8, 13; Ben Simmons, p. 5 (2nd from top), II: 2, 3, 10, 13, 27; IV: 2, 3, 4, 5; Summer Art Festival in Hakushu, IV: 10; Yutaka Suzuki, p. 4, II: 4, 21, 23, 39; Shiro Takatani, IV: 6; Toshinobu Takeuchi, I: 9, 15, 45, 46, 47; Yasutake Tanji, I: 6; Hiroshi Tonoshiro, p. 2; Ryuzo Toyotaka, back jacket, I: 12, 21; II: 14; David Wade, II: 11, 24, 37; III: 1; Manabu Watanabe, III: 15; Yuzo Yamada, II: 20, 49; Ikio Yamamoto, II: 31; Hiroaki Yamashita, I: 22; Mike Yamashita, p. 5 (3rd from top), II: 40; Akinobu Yanagi, I: 5; Hiroshi Yokoyama, I: 11; Chiaki Yoshida, III: 2, 3.

ACKNOWLEDGMENTS

Naojiro Ando; Chusonji; Daisen'in; Dandy Photo; Geographic Photo; Geijutsu Shincho/Shinchosha; Haga Library; Himeji Castle; Horyuji; Ikenobo; Imperial Household Agency; Ise Shrine; Japan Sports; Japan Stage Players' Association; Japan Sumo Association; Kanshinji; Machiko Kobayashi; Kodaiji; Myokian; Shin'ichi Nakajima; Ryoichi Nakamura; Nijo Castle; Pacific Press Service; Q Photo International; RETORIA; Shirakawa-go Kanko Kyokai; Sogetsukai Foundation; Sojiji; Todaiji; Urasenke.

Distributed in the United States by Kodansha America, Inc., 575 Lexington Avenue, New York, New York 10022, and in the United Kingdom and continental Europe by Kodansha Europe Ltd., 95 Aldwych, London WC2B 4JF.

Published by Kodansha International Ltd., 17–14 Otowa 1-chome, Bunkyo-ku, Tokyo 112–8652, and Kodansha America, Inc.

Copyright © 1994 and 1999 by Kodansha International Ltd. All rights reserved. Printed in China.

First edition, 1994
Revised edition, 1999
01 02 03   5 4

ISBN 4-7700-2478-9

www.thejapanpage.com

C O N T E N T S

Japan: An Exotic Land, A Modern Land

JAPAN INTRIGUED ME THE FIRST TIME I caught sight of it and it still intrigues me today. We are always hearing that Japan is a land of contrasts—and it certainly is. Over the past few decades these contrasts, instead of diminishing with Japan's modernization and Westernization, have in my opinion grown sharper. Wherever you go in Japan—to the snowy northern island of Hokkaido or to the southern extreme in tropical Okinawa—the contrasts are there. You will see centuries-old tradition existing side-by-side with the latest in modern technology. In the same location you will see the most Western of office buildings right next to purely Japanese structures. And as the readers of this wonderful book will see, the setting for this exotic land of contrasts is one of the most lovely natural environments in the world.

My long acquaintance with Japan began in 1922 when I first caught sight of the country from the deck of a troop ship. Our port of call, Nagasaki, had a great impact on me. I was a Marine aged only nineteen then and not long away from home in Montana. What I saw was a beautiful natural setting. I was to see Japan often in the years after that first encounter but it was the first glimpse—of the rugged coastline, the dozens of islands dotting the approach to the harbor and the exotic sights of the town itself that made the greatest impression.

Thankfully, the port of Nagasaki maintains much of its original character. It was the destruction of Nagasaki by an American atomic bomb in 1945 that finally forced Japan's Imperial government to surrender to the Allies. Rebuilt along modern lines but retaining the best of its Japanese traditions, today's Nagasaki has the same exotic charm that had attracted me many decades ago.

My next encounter with Japan was in the immediate aftermath of World War II. As a Congressman from Montana, I was sent to Japan to survey the war damage and evaluate our plans to restore Japan to prosperity and full membership in the world community. What I saw was devastation. Whole cities had been reduced to rubble. Food was very scarce. Social services—education, medical care, transportation—were minimal or nonexistent. But I noticed that the people were up to the challenge of survival and I felt sure that Japan's resilient and cohesive population would win that struggle decisively.

The six long years of occupation by the Allied powers which followed were in many ways a period of renewal and reform. Advised by progressive Japanese experts, the Allies made major reforms: land reform loosened the monopoly over agricultural production held by landlords; educational reform opened higher education to all, including women; labor reform made unions and collective bargaining legal; women were made full citizens and given the right to vote. Most important was the establishment of a democratic constitution with a legislature, political parties, and periodic elections. Together, these reforms laid the basis for Japan's tremendous social and economic progress in the postwar period.

I visited Japan several times during the 1960s and 1970s. What I saw was growth. The energy, determination, and skill of the Japanese people were tremendous. Japan's hardworking population benefited from one of the world's best education systems. Japanese society gained stability from responsive, democratic government on the national and local levels. An honest and well-organized civil service brought impartial government administration to all corners of the country. A free press gave active coverage to all segments of opinion. Prosperous and confident, many Japanese went abroad as students, businessmen, and tourists. And the world came to Japan, not only as tourists but also as students of that exotic culture and its very difficult language. Some of the young scholars and businessmen who went to Japan in those years have since come to fulfill important liaison roles in interpreting and explaining Japan to the West.

As the economy grew by leaps and bounds and Japan's export products began competing successfully in international markets, the world awoke to the presence of a major new power. However, this prosperity and progress had its negative side: in some ways the growth had been too fast. In the 1960s and early 1970s, little attention was being paid to the noneconomic impact of such tremendous development. Cities had become overcrowded. Traffic jams were commonplace, and housing was scarce and of poor quality. Water, electricity, and gas distribution was inadequate. Pollution from the many new factories degraded the air quality and damaged some of Japan's natural beauty.

In 1977, I became American Ambassador to Japan. What I saw during these years was a rising standard of living. As citizens came to realize that there was more to their lives than just cash income, the tide began to turn. With a new focus on the quality of life, the Japanese people began the slow process of restoring the environment and upgrading the nation's social infrastructure.

Fortunately, most of the environmental damage was reversible and the results have been excellent. For example, the Tama River on the southern border of the Tokyo metropolis at one time had become so heavily polluted that its salmon all but disappeared. The river was cleaned up, and the salmon have now returned. In the same way, strict auto emission controls have been successful in reducing air pollution in Japan's crowded urban areas.

As the readers of this thoughtfully compiled book will see, today's Japan retains all of the special flavor that attracted me so many years ago. Japan is the modern, impressive Westernized nation whose trade with the rest of the world has an immediate impact on all of us, and at the same time it remains an exotic nation with roots still deep in the traditions of its unique past. As Japan continues to grow in importance to the rest of the world, the need for people familiar with its customs, religion, economy, politics, and culture will increase. My hope is that many who read this book will be attracted to Japan, as I was, and will be motivated to learn more about that very special country.

Mike Mansfield

Youngsters in Hiroshima appeal for peace in front of the Atomic Bomb Dome, the skeletal remains of a building destroyed by atomic bombing in World War II.

A view of Nagasaki harbor. Nagasaki has survived the ravages of war, and is today a thriving center for shipbuilding, deep-sea fishing, and other industries.

Harmonizing with Nature

by Dorothy Britton

What better symbol for Japan than this magnificent mountain! Fuji dominates both land and people. More often hidden than seen, its varied aspects never fail to astound. The most blasé taxi driver invariably turns his head to see if Fuji is there. A jaded commuter hopes to catch a glimpse of it as his bullet train whizzes by. Japanese artists down the ages have spent their lives trying to capture Fuji's multitude of faces. And if "Rain obscures the scene," as 17th-century poet Basho wrote, "Fuji still exerts a charm / Even when unseen!"

The fact that Fuji is a volcano, erupting every few centuries, heightens its mystique, and serves as a constant reminder how unstable this archipelago is. Hence the sense of impermanence that pervades Japanese literature and thought. Even the deity Fuji enshrines—the Goddess of Flowering Trees—is associated with the fleeting, fragile beauty of cherry blossoms.

Fuji is a sacred mountain. One of the many numinous regions in this scenic wonderland, Fuji is where the ancients who founded the Shinto faith felt a specially awe-inspiring awareness of a divine presence. It is to be approached with purity of heart and mind and body.

"May all six of my senses be pure; may the weather be fair on the Mountain!" earnestly chant the white-clad pilgrims—some in their eighties and even blind—as they plod up Fuji's trails with their tinkling bells and staves in July and August. They are jostled by boys who hump bicycles up the arduous trail for the fun and challenge of riding them around the perilous crater rim, and throngs of other less religious hikers who are nonetheless awed by the sunrise, and say a prayer at the summit shrine.

The view from the summit of row upon row of mountain ranges melting into the far distance reveals how Japan—little bigger than Britain—is four-fifths mountainous with only a bare 20 percent flat enough for habitation. The one large plain encompassing Tokyo and Yokohama must accommodate so much ugly industrial activity that it is scarcely relieved by any greenery. That is what visitors see first, and wonder what became of Japan's celebrated natural beauty.

The mountains have been its savior—the deeply forested slopes too steep for the greedy bulldozer that has, alas, devoured or flattened too many green foothills.

On a clear day, snow-capped Mt. Fuji, looking like the tip of a far-off mound of sugar, peers between skyscrapers to remind one that verdant forests and ravines full of gurgling brooks and birdsong await the enterprising traveler, along with many fascinating protected seascapes. Like Fuji, Japan's beauty is not always immediately visible, but is there for the seeking, in amazing diversity.

1. Mt. Fuji, Japan's highest mountain (3,776 meters), soars in solitary splendor from a coastal plain. Seemingly a perfect cone, Fuji has a flawed symmetry that only adds to its fascination. A dormant volcano, Fuji last erupted in 1707.

Hokkaido: Snowy Home of the Ainu and Japanese Crane

The tunnel connecting Honshu to Hokkaido is still the longest in the world, although its undersea portion is slightly shorter than that of the new English Channel tunnel. But whether you cross the stormy strait by train, air or ferry, you will seem to have reached a different country altogether. The wide plains and gentle hills, with their farms, dairies, vineyards, and American-style clapboarded buildings with mansard roofs conform to a pattern introduced little more than a century ago when an attempt was made to populate the island. Until then, except for political exiles who founded a samurai fief at its southernmost tip, the subarctic climate had repelled the Japanese. The region was home mainly to the Ainu, the indigenous Ural-Altaic people who once inhabited much of the main island, Honshu, until driven north.

Still sparsely populated, Hokkaido's crystalline lakes and mountains have a grandeur all their own. Mt. Daisetsu's highest peak, though only 2,290 meters high, boasts an extinct crater two kilometers in diameter and flora and fauna of great interest and diversity. New volcanoes made startling appearances in 1910 and 1943, the latter being one of the world's youngest.

Kushiro Marsh, east Hokkaido's vast wetland, is now a national park. It is home to the elegantly beautiful red-crowned cranes, which breed in the summer marshes and gather on snow-covered farmland in winter, where feeding programs are gradually restoring their numbers.

2. Fields of variegated barley at a farm in Bieicho, central Hokkaido.

3. Red-crowned cranes (*Grus japonensis*) love to dance—as much from pure joie de vivre, as when courting. Kushiro Marsh and some nearby wetlands are now the only Japanese habitat of this elegant bird, symbol of good fortune, longevity, and marital bliss.

4. Often cradling fleecy mists in summer, Akan National Park's deep crater lake, Mashu, is one of the world's clearest. Its steep sides are thickly forested, and a lava dome breaking the surface is called by the Ainu "The Isle of the Gods."

3

4

Tohoku: Once Rugged Frontier Country

Honshu, Japan's largest main island, is shaped rather like a boomerang, with one wing running northeast and the other southwest. They are divided from one another by the "Fossa Magna" fault and the Fuji volcanic chain. The two wings are further separated by geological and climatic conditions that make up five districts that are quite distinct, both physically and culturally.

Long considered the "back of beyond," and still rustic and undeveloped, Tohoku—the northeastern wing—has two faces: the bleak Japan Sea coast, snowbound for months, and the more temperate shores along the Pacific Ocean. The craggy, spectacular Pacific coast is protected from the icy Siberian winds by a mountain spine that contains a virgin beech forest designated a world heritage by UNESCO, and two national parks: one featuring eight dormant volcanoes and a picturesque lake that is one of Japan's three deepest, and the other a holy trinity of peaks known as Dewa Sanzan, home to an ancient ascetic mountain cult.

The cold side along the Japan Sea is famed for its lovely peaches-and-cream-complexioned women, its luscious apples and sake, its lilting folk tunes and virtuoso style of playing the three-stringed *shamisen*. The warmer side revels in vivid gorges and romantic seascapes like "Paradise Beach," with its gleaming white quartz rocks embellished with graceful pines.

5

5. Fantastic sea-eroded rock towers and grottoes extend for miles along the northern part of the Rikuchu Coast National Park.

6. A UNESCO-listed virgin forest of Japanese beech (*Fagus crenata*) in the Shirakami Mountains.

7. An 11-kilometer path winding through the Oirase River Valley provides charming vistas of waterfalls, rapids, mossy boulders, and wooded cliffs. The Oirase's source is Lake Towada, focal point of the Towada-Hachimantai National Park.

6

7

Kanto: The Bustling Center of Japan

The great metropolis of Tokyo and its six surrounding home counties comprise the district known as Kanto, meaning "East of the Barrier." It was frontier country in earlier times, when Kyoto was the hub and an important checkpoint near Lake Biwa indicated the boundary between civilization and regions beyond. Kanto today is hardly the "wild east." Occupying the largest plain in the country, it is Japan's most densely populated area and not only its economic, political, and industrial center, but now its cultural heartland too.

Development began in the 12th century when the shoguns set up military rule in Kamakura. Then in 1603, the great Tokugawa Ieyasu chose Edo (now Tokyo) for his castle seat, with great plans for this eastern region. Nikko was to be its religious center, and he was buried here, amid the awesome forest of giant cryptomerias that today enshroud the sky-blue, gingko-gold and maple-leaf vermilion carvings of his gorgeous mausoleum, the Toshogu shrine. A wonderland of mountains, waterfalls, and lakes, Nikko can be reached from Tokyo in under two hours. Conservationists have succeeded in preserving the magnificent tree-lined way leading to the shrine, as well as an outstanding highland marsh at Oze, not far away.

And metropolitan Tokyo, believe it or not, administers a series of islands that march southwards in single file down into the sub-tropical Pacific all the way to Iojima, or "sulfur island," known in the West as Iwo Jima.

8. Mountain-encircled Oze Marsh, 1,400 meters up in the Nikko Highlands, is ablaze in summer with orange day lilies. Wooden walkways provide access to this important protected wetland, rich in a variety of plants, birds, and insects.

9. Water left by heavy rain mirrors a forest of larch at the edge of Odashirogahara, a grassy plain in the Nikko Highlands.

10. The Ogasawara National Park, one of Japan's smallest and newest, mainly comprises the Ogasawara Islands, with their white-sand beaches and semi-tropical jungle. Once known as the Bonin ("uninhabited") Islands, they were first settled in 1830 by a handful of American, British and Hawaiian whalers. The Park also includes North Iojima, a spectacular sulfurous cone.

9

10

Chubu: Mountaineering Paradise

Mt. Fuji is the pride of the mountainous Central Region, or Chubu, that encompasses numerous ranges culminating in the Japan Alps. All three of the nation's holiest peaks are here: Fuji, Tateyama, and Hakusan, each within a national park.

Japan's sacred mountains were consecrated for pilgrimage by pioneering monks over a thousand years ago, but it was a British missionary, Walter Weston—an experienced alpinist—who led the way here for climbing as a sport. In a book published in 1896 he wrote, "The Japanese Alps are now without glaciers, and their scale is only about two-thirds of the European Alps. But the ravines in the Japanese Alps are like paintings, rich with color, and the splendid calm of the dense woods covering the mountainsides exceeds any other scenery which I have ever seen while wandering in the European Alps."

Mt. Hakusan, near the snowy Japan Sea coast, looks down upon Kanazawa, an elegant castle town known for its water garden and Kutani-ware kilns, and the Noto Peninsula, famous for its Wajima lacquerware. Mt. Tateyama casts a benign eye on Takayama, a miniature Kyoto deep in the Hida Range, which boasts one of the most spectacular festivals in Japan, featuring a parade of elaborate 16th-century wagon floats.

11

12

13

11. The rising sun emblazons Tateyama's peaks to match the autumnal tints of trees fringing Sennin-ike, the "Lake of the Mountain Wizard."

12. Known as Tojimbo, these pillars of volcanic rock resembling Northern Ireland's "Giant's Causeway" are among the dramatic features of the spectacular Japan Sea coast off Fukui Prefecture.

13. Tsurugidake ("Sword Peak") in the Japan Alps, seen at dawn, with a covering of new snow. It claims a height of 2,998 meters, and a blade-sharp ridge that makes it a popular challenge to alpinists.

Kinki: Repository of Culture and History

The old designation Kansai, or "West of the Barrier," is still widely used to refer to the area around Osaka, Kyoto, and Kobe, now known officially as the Kinki region. Its distinctive soft speech (*Kansai-ben*), food, and customs have a special charm. This is the ancient cultural heart of Japan, centered around the old capitals Nara and Kyoto, where the emperors had their palaces and where religion, art, and literature flourished.

Kyoto straddles the pellucid Kamo River, near lute-shaped Lake Biwa, the largest lake in Japan. The awe-inspiring Ise Shrine, dedicated to the Sun Goddess and built anew every 20 years, is nearby on the Kii Peninsula, as is Mt. Koya with its venerable Buddhist monasteries. The shrine and monasteries stand amid magnificent cedar forests of *Cryptomeria japonica*.

Yoshinoyama is famed for the thousands of wild cherry trees covering its hills in springtime with clouds of pale pink blossoms. Oft alluded to in the *Manyoshu*, or "Ten Thousand Leaves"—the amazing 8th-century anthology of 4,500 poems written by prince and peasant alike—these venerable hills are today part of the Yoshino-Kumano National Park. Also found in this park are virgin forests, a holy waterfall, caves where a 14th-century emperor once took refuge, and a cape where a strange procession of giant rocks shaped like cowled monks marches out into the waves. Tradition says this sea-eroded shale ridge once supported a bridge built in a single night by a 9th-century priest eager to reach an offshore island to pray for souls lost at sea.

14

14. Wild cherry trees bloom in succession all April on Yoshinoyama, eight kilometers of hills near Nara. "Oh, oh, oh! / Wordless was I when I saw / The trees at Yoshino," wrote haiku poet Teishitsu (1609–1673).

15. A tranquil sunset scene on Lake Biwa ("Lute Lake"). At the tip of its "neck" lies Otsu, once a 7th-century capital, but now an industrial city near Kyoto. Many old prints depict the lake's "Eight Scenic Spots." Trout and carp are fished, and freshwater pearls cultivated here.

16. Majestic Nachi Falls, thundering down through a numinous forest, is awe-inspiring in the extreme. The ancients sensed the presence of deity here and built a shrine at its feet.

15

16

Chugoku and Shikoku: Embracing the Inland Sea

Chugoku, the "Middle Provinces," form a fan-like arc at Honshu's western extremity, with Australia-shaped four-province Shikoku—Japan's smallest main island—just below. Between them lies the beautiful Inland Sea, with its whirlpools and myriad pine-clad isles.

This is where Japanese civilization began to take shape. According to one theory, invading tribes from the continent arrived in Japan via Korea early in the Christian era. Some settled in the Izumo Plain on the northern coast, leaving us the ancient Izumo Shrine and a host of myths and legends. Others, after a sojourn in Kyushu, moved gradually eastward along the Inland Sea, where they were so awe-inspired by the island of Miyajima that their descendants built a remarkable shrine there, right out into the water. These people finally settled in the Yamato Plain at the Sea's eastern end, establishing the dominant court in Nara.

Much of the Inland Sea is now a national park, while east of Izumo two sections of the Japan Sea side are similarly protected: 1,711-meter Mt. Daisen and the offshore Oki Islands with their multihued cliffs, and 77 kilometers of coast celebrated for its fantastic rock formations—a veritable museum of sea sculpture—and sand dunes and lagoons unknown on the Pacific side of Japan. Although, sadly, a good half of this country's picturesque coastline has been commercially developed, it is fortunate that at least a dozen sections have been preserved for their diversity as spectacular national parks.

17

17. The still picturesque Inland Sea was made a National Park in 1934 to keep pollution in check when industrialization began. Some of its myriad islands are connected now to the mainland with graceful, high-tech bridges.

18. The Tottori dunes were formed by fine sand from the Sendai riverbed, washed out to sea and then cast up on the Japan Sea shore by currents and high waves. Strong Siberian winds finally blew the sand into these great furrowed heaps.

19. This "Buddhist statue" Kannon-iwa, named after the Goddess of Mercy, is one of many eroded sandstone formations in the Ashizuri-Uwakai National Park on Shikoku's western coast. Other fantastic shapes include the giant "bamboo skewers" of Tatsukushi, or "Dragon Shishkebab."

20. The "Hundred Saucers" of Akiyoshido, one of the largest limestone caves in the world. At a depth of almost a kilometer, the cave contains rivers, waterfalls, and deep pools, as well as columns, stalactites and stalagmites.

18

19

20

Kyushu: Where the Gods Descended

Joined to Honshu by a bridge over the merest of straits, Kyushu—the third largest and southernmost of Japan's main islands—has the biggest volcanic crater basin in the world, containing five peaks, two valleys, three villages and three towns. One peak is active, but the people have learned to live with it. So have those who live at the very base of another volcano, Sakurajima, located right in the middle of Kagoshima Bay at Kyushu's southern tip. It erupts often, and rumbles all the time. But the eruption that took people by surprise in 1991 was that of Mt. Unzen. Known for its spas, Unzen was the scene of 17th-century Christian martyrdoms in its bubbling pools.

It must have been Mt. Kirishima's lush slopes, resplendent with *Rhododendron kiusianum*, that seduced the Yamato tribesmen before they set off north-eastwards, taking with them the Sun Goddess myth. According to the myth, it is 1,574-meter Takachiho, on Kirishima's southern edge, upon which the grandson of the Sun Goddess descended from heaven to found the Imperial line—the world's oldest.

Seventy kilometers south of Kyushu is the remarkable, circular island of Yakushima, only 100 kilometers around but almost 2,000 meters high. It is famous for its *Jomon sugi*—giant ancient cedars awarded world heritage status by UNESCO—and its dramatic range of plant life, from subtropical to alpine, that makes it a horticulturist's dream.

Yakushima is the first of a series of islands reaching south to balmy Iriomote in the Okinawa chain, just one degree north of the Tropic of Cancer.

21

21. The world's largest volcano, Mt. Aso, whose lava has covered most of Kyushu. Mt. Aso's caldera, with a circumference of 80 kilometers, contains five craters, but only Naka-dake ("Inner Peak") is still active. On safe days, one can peer down at the wisps of smoke rising from its vividly striated depths.

22. One of the cedars (*Cryptomeria japonica*) of immense girth and age, halfway up the mountainous island of Yakushima. Possibly 1,000 to 2,000 years old, they are traditionally supposed to date back to Japan's neolithic Jomon Period.

23. A magnificent coral reef rims an aquamarine lagoon off the sparkling Shiraho beach of Ishigakijima, part of the Okinawa island chain. Environmentalists are trying to save this reef, whose wonders include rare blue coral (*Heliopora coerulea*).

22

23

II

TODAY'S JAPANESE

A Yen for Perfection and Prosperity

by Frederick Hiroshi Katayama

Japan works. Subway riders patiently wait in lines; trains come on time. The milk carton opens at the folds, and soda machines dispense the exact amount of change. Japan's industrious work force ensures these little pleasantries with its devotion to detail and obsession with quality.

To get a glimpse of contemporary life in Japan, venture into a department store on a weekend just as it opens for business. The uniformed troops of sales attendants bow deeply and greet shoppers with choruses of "Irasshaimase!" (Welcome!) You wiggle your way through crowds so thick you would think it's a clearance sale. Ask for that blue skirt in red, and the saleslady flashes a quick smile before scampering off for the stockroom.

But check the price tag, and you'll discover that despite the appearances, the customer isn't king—this is a producer-led, consumer-fed society. What's more, services Westerners would consider extraneous, even humorous, such as the white-gloved elevator operators with their robotized monologues, keep customers pampered but operating costs high.

You'll also notice that most shoppers pay for their wares in cash. Consumers don't worry about carrying wads of yen because the streets are relatively safe. Unlike their counterparts in much of the industrialized world, kids with their boxy backpacks walk home from school unaccompanied; their mothers can walk unescorted among the twisty back roads at night, even in Tokyo. Foreign residents regale in telling tales of losing their purses, only to recover them with cash and cards intact.

With so much of the population crammed in urban areas—more than 40 percent of the national populace lives in Tokyo, Osaka and Nagoya—the cities set the country's trends and pump out popular culture. Much of that is geared to Japan's prodigal young, such as the insipid but innocuous top-40ish, bubble gum pop. Tokyo's teens and twenty-somethings exhibit an insatiable appetite for anything new; smash-hit products have been made out of items ranging from Australian frilled lizards to the Italian dessert tiramisu.

But with one of the lowest birthrates in the world, Japan will gray faster than any other industrialized nation. And witness the countryside. Urbanization has left it disproportionately populated with the Geritol generation. Kids graduate from school and grab a one-way ticket to the cities. In the 1960s, the middle class scrimped and saved so they could afford the "3Cs": air conditioner, car, and color TV. Today, young Japanese want to avoid labor-intensive jobs like farming and fishing, as greater numbers leave the good earth for the great megalopolis.

1. The world's most popular sport recently swept into Japan, and it has whipped up a colorful frenzy among sports fanatics and the corporations that sponsor the teams. Fortunately, it hasn't spawned hooliganism.

Tokyo: Heartbeat of Japan

Japan is a one-city country. Tokyo dominates. After all, the Tokyo metropolitan area houses 32 percent of Japan's population. Pick up a magazine, and chances are, all but perhaps one or two of the restaurants and shops featured are located in Tokyo. It's the capital of commerce, the creator of trends, and the command post from which Japan's mighty mandarins rule. Tokyo's baseball team, the Giants, are to the Japanese what the New York Yankees are to Americans.

Buzzwords come and go; buildings sprout and succumb in this fickle metropolis. But old and new coexist side-by-side. Hidden amidst the skyscrapers of Shinjuku are old shrines. Akihabara showcases the latest high-tech toys, while just a mile away, a tidy shop in Nihombashi sells what it's been selling for almost three centuries: wooden toothpicks. In the suburbs, a shiny Benz breezes past a septuagenarian vendor who pushes a smoky wooden cart loaded with stone-baked sweet potatoes.

The drab concrete slabs rob Marunouchi, Tokyo's business district, of the grandeur and glitter that garnish Manhattan or the stately elegance of London. Never mind, for the lordly Imperial fortress nearby lends it the luster of history and pride. Better yet, there's the majestic view of Mt. Fuji on a clear day. Marunouchi, the peak, and the palace are constant reminders of the unofficial motto of corporate Japan: "for company, for country."

2

3

2. The symbol of the country, the Emperor, lives with his family beyond the moat in the Imperial Palace set in the heart of Tokyo.

3. Until a cluster of skyscrapers took root in western Shinjuku, many urban observers claimed Tokyo was a city without a skyline. Yet for others, views are abundant. Here, a quiet evening's illumination, with Tokyo Tower in the foreground, soothes the eye.

Japan's Corporate Creed: Working Nine to Nine

He's a foot soldier of the corporate army that contributed to Japan's phoenix-like ascendance out of the ashes. He is the salaryman, the white-collared workhorse who toils in a smoke-filled office by day and swigs and sings for his sale with clients at a *karaoke* bar by night. Liquor, it's said, lubricates the senses and fosters human relations, the core to doing business in Japan. With his blue suit, white shirt and striped tie, he could just as well be working for IBM. You're apt to see him downing a brown-bottled pep drink or swinging an imaginary golf club while waiting for his train. But there's a dark side to his slavish devotion to work. Many overstressed workaholics have fallen victim to *karoshi*, death by overwork:

Women working for corporations are more likely than not "OLs," short for office ladies, Japan's uniformed secretarial troops who pour tea, make copies, and answer phones. Women grabbed headlines in the late 1980s when many companies began hiring them for managerial tracks, all in the name of equal opportunity. But good will wasn't the reason, for corporate Japan was simply entangled in a labor shortage amidst the economic boom. When boom turned to bust, companies cut back more heavily on women recruits than male college grads.

However, given that Japan's rapidly aging society will generate an acute labor shortage over the next few decades, companies will be on the lookout for more women. Just think: when management fully taps its long underemployed talent pool, corporate Japan could become even mightier.

4

5

6

4. These office lights will burn late into the night, for Japan's corporate warriors are among the world's hardest working people.

5. The nation's legion of salarymen and "OLs" get ready for another hard day of work.

6. The Shinkansen bullet train streaks past some of the world's priciest property. One square meter in the Ginza entertainment district pictured here can cost as much as $275,000.

7. Rush-hour on a train platform. Trains are so packed that the government has a new goal: easing congestion so straphangers can comfortably read a newspaper.

8. Enjoing the after-hours: a cosy couple displays the social influence of the West at this nighttime alley in Shinjuku. Kissing in public, however, is frowned upon.

9. Many businessmen work off stress at bars and restaurants like this outdoor *yakitori* (barbecued chicken) stall before heading home.

7

8

9

Tokyo Living: Home in a High-Rise

On the surface, the average Japanese household resembles the type of family featured in a 1950s TV sitcom: a nuclear household with two kids and two parents. Mom is the homemaker; papa, the breadwinner.

But the similarities end there. Japanese typically live in cramped high-rises about an hour's commute from the office. Pop doesn't come home at six. He'll slug down a few beers and croon some tunes at a bar with colleagues or clients at night. But nowadays young fathers like him are more family-oriented than their dads. He'll try to spend Sunday at home.

Mom runs the house. She cooks, cleans, tutors the kids, and manages the budget. But unlike her house-bound mother, she'll help out at the neighborhood supermarket or hold a job at a local boutique—yet get home in time to prepare supper. Over half of young mothers in Japan work part-time. The 80s saw the arrival of some DINKs (double-income, no kids) on the urban scene, one of the many trends that may spell change for families of the future.

For the youngsters, it's late to bed, early to rise, make the kid study, all ears and eyes. Unlike Tommy, Taro doesn't have to mow the lawn, as that would rob him of time better spent preparing for college entrance exams. But once inside the university gates like his older brother Ichiro, Taro's more likely to play tennis than pore through Plato, for college will be his last chance to have fun before he sells his soul to corporate Japan. According to one tale, two-thirds of the class at an elite Tokyo college failed the first question of their final exam. It featured three snapshots. The question: which one is your teacher?

10. In the dense urban congestion of Tokyo, high-rise complexes are home to many. The monorail that runs between Haneda Airport and Hamamatsucho Station on Tokyo Bay provides access to the city center.

11. The Japanese call it "family service." Fathers take time out on the weekends to play with their kids. Workaholic dads hardly see them during the week.

12. Rows of shops are a common sight around suburban railway stations. Housewives usually shop for fresh foodstuffs everyday, partly because their small kitchens won't accommodate a week's worth of food.

13. Eating is one of Japan's favorite pastimes, and a highlight of many family outings is *gaishoku*, a meal out on the town. Here diners gather at the counter of a popular "conveyer-belt sushi bar."

11

12

13

Working Hard at Leisure

In the golden days of the Heian period (794–1195), courtiers scribbled love poems on fans to wile away idleness. In the get-ahead, make-some-bread 20th century, Japanese should take a lesson from their noble ancestors, for if there's one thing they're not good at, it's leisure (well, with the exception of college students).

That's changing, albeit slowly. Some major companies coax their workers to take time off, and the government has cut school hours and pledged to shorten working hours. Young workers value their private life more than their professional life, the reverse of what their elders felt. They've added to their lexicon *hana no kinyobi*, Japanese for TGIF. Impatient workers celebrate *hana moku*, i.e., TGI Thursday.

Considering the abundance of restaurants—Tokyo boasts more per capita than any other city—it's no wonder that eating out is the leading leisure activity. The big up-and-comer: *karaoke*, or singing to the accompaniment of recorded background music à la Mitch Miller. Among spectator sports, the 2,000 year-old granddaddy, sumo, has made a resurgence, aided by the rise of American wrestlers. The world's most popular sport, soccer, is on its way to becoming a hit here as well. The trendy treasure tennis and skiing, but don't let those Rossignol skis and Prince rackets fool you: those sporting the trophy brands are often beginners who want to socialize on the slopes and court off the court.

14

14. Traffic "dam": public pools get so packed in the summer that swimmers can only afford to do the breast stroke to avoid bumping into each other.

15. Golfers practice at this rooftop range in the Ginza. Some never make it to the links because a round of 18 at $300 is out of their price range.

16. One of every four Japanese play *pachinko*, the Japanese version of pinball, on a regular basis. Pinball wizards redeem the metal balls for prizes, although some illegally trade for cash instead.

17. At Sega Enterprises' high-tech amusement center, this racetrack game offers the thrills of a Las Vegas casino.

18. While soccer has garnered much of the spotlight in recent years, it is baseball, which the Japanese took up in the late 1880s, that reigns as the country's most popular team sport.

15

16

17

18

Life in the Past Lane

Tokyo retains traces of the past as it unsentimentally races for the future. Just look at the streets. Fires and earthquakes, not to mention a war, gave city planners a chance to redesign the landscape, but Tokyo is still bric-a-block with narrow, sinuous streets and cul-de-sacs…great for deterring invading warriors in days gone by, and fun for walking, but a pain for driving.

Despite their love of things new, Tokyoites revere the past. On New Year's Day, crowds flock to the Buddhist temple Sensoji in the old Asakusa district. This centerpiece of Asakusa hails back to the 7th century. Along the arcade in the temple grounds, a merchant selling cheap souvenirs competes for the yen of tourists with a vendor who nervously flips metal molds to make *ningyoyaki*, a sweet confection filled with red bean paste. Not far away, the

toasty aroma of soy sauce wafts from a shop where another vendor hand-roasts rice crackers called *sembei*. Also in this part of *shitamachi*—as the old merchants' districts of the city are called—are theaters where professional storytellers, *rakugoka*, entertain audiences with their yarn, continuing a tradition stretching back to the 17th century.

If you're lucky, you might catch sight (certainly your ears will) of the *chin-don'ya*. Though dwindling in number, a few of these gaudily dressed entertainers still parade the streets, banging gongs and plucking the *shamisen* to plug grand openings of stores and other events in the neighborhood.

19   20

19. Located in the urban jungle, Meiji Shrine offers tranquillity and exudes a spiritual aura. Just outside the grounds, foppish youngsters dance to the beat of street musicians on Sundays.

20. The spirit of the old districts known as *shitamachi* comes alive during Asakusa's Sanja festival. People parade 100 portable shrines called *mikoshi* up and down the streets.

21. Visitors at the Edo-Tokyo Museum get a feel of what Tokyo looked like before modernity set in.

22. Worshipers smother themselves with incense at the temple Sensoji in the belief that this will dispel them of illness and disease.

23. While Americans stay home on New Year's to watch college football on TV, Japanese ring in the year by visiting a temple or shrine. A New Year's street performer greets a youngster at the Ikegami Honmonji temple.

24. Only the walkway and mini "gardens" of potted plants separate these homes in this *shitamachi* district. Unlike many high-rise condo dwellers, people in these communities know their neighbors.

21

22

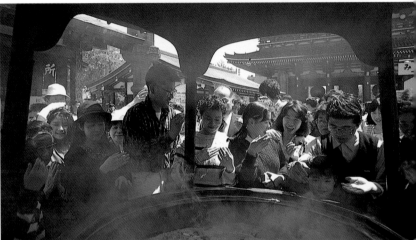

23

24

A Treasure of Pleasures Just Outside Tokyo

All roads don't lead to Tokyo, but roads from Tokyo can lead to many a pleasant, nearby getaway. Just 45 kilometers southwest lies Kamakura, the lush seaside city that was once Japan's medieval capital. It teems with temples and shrines that are encased by heavily forested mountains. Casting a serene meditative aura over Kamakura is the Daibutsu. Japan's second largest bronze Buddha sits peacefully in the open air nestled in the hills, keeping watch over the surfers at Sagami Bay.

"If you haven't seen Nikko, you can't say *kekko.*" "*Kekko*" means you're satisfied, and most visitors to Nikko are. Dating back to the 17th century, the Toshogu shrine in Nikko shocks the senses of Japanophiles who cherish the country's aesthetic of restraint. Its ornately carved gate, Yomeimon, is also known as the "Higurashinomon," or Twilight Gate, ostensibly because the awe-struck will gawk at it 'til dusk. One of Japan's most famous waterfalls, Kegon Falls, also commands respect. Originating from Lake Chuzenji, it gushes straight down the length of a football field (90 meters) against a forest of green that turns into a quilt of pastel colors in the fall.

Yokohama, Japan's second largest city, is just half-an-hour away from Tokyo by train. As if to boast that it's second to none, Yokohama has built Japan's tallest skyscraper, the glittery, 296-meter-high Landmark Tower housing 190 tony boutiques and restaurants.

25

26

27

25. Japan's tallest tower, the lavish Landmark Tower in Yokohama, is awesome, but it doesn't elicit as many ahs as the country's most famous landmark, Mt. Fuji.

26. Street stalls selling steamed pork buns are a fixture of Chinatowns from San Francisco to this one in Yokohama.

27. Sidewalk surfin': Japanese beach bums like this Shonan surfer will do whatever it takes to get their surfboards to shore—whether by car, train or even bike.

28. Visitors gawk at the elaborate carvings of Nikko's Toshogu.

29. Along with cherry blossoms and Mt. Fuji, one of the pre-eminent symbols of Japan is the giant Buddha in Kamakura.

28

29

Kyoto: A Museum of Culture

At first glance, Kyoto might elicit blahs instead of ahs. It's geographically flat and visually dull. Streets stretch out in plain checkerboard fashion. Kyoto lacks the spiralling skyscrapers of Tokyo, the greenery of Nikko, the rambunctious spirit of Osaka.

But many of the cultural assets of this ancient capital—it's home to one-fifth of the national treasures—lay incognito behind the walls of its 2,000 temples and shrines. Kyoto is a 1,200-year-old museum. It's no wonder that each year, more than 38 million tourists—almost tantamount to the population of Spain—trample its walks.

The hordes of visitors can rob the city of the pleasures of serenity and the ascetic tranquillity expressed in the tea ceremony and flower arrangement, both of which originated in Kyoto. To experience the Zen spirit of quiescence, many turn to the raked rock garden of Ryoanji, said to evoke an ocean filled with islands—but it's so austere any imaginary waves are more likely to be ripples.

You would be lucky if you ran into a geisha along your strolls through the ancient alleyways, for there are fewer of them around these days. Many Japanese businessmen today prefer to drink at nightclubs with coquettish hostesses than at teahouses with these entertainers of old. The "flower-and-willow world" of the geisha slowly wilts with the passage of time.

30

31

33

30. Kyoto's Gion Matsuri is arguably Japan's greatest festival. Almost as old as Kyoto itself, the festival was begun in 869 in the hopes that the gods would eliminate an epidemic.

31. In the Aoi Festival, men dressed as ancient nobles tow a cart adorned with the leaves of the *aoi* (wild ginger) plant as they march from Kyoto's Imperial Palace to the two Kamo Shrines.

32. An elegant geisha strolls through the narrow passageways, or *roji*, in the Ginza of geisha districts, Gion.

33. Geisha are dispatched to *ochaya*, or teahouses, like these along the Shirakawa Canal in Gion.

32

Life in Kyoto: The Past in the Present

Kyotoites have a reputation for being a smug lot, somewhat akin to the Brahmins of Boston, which—you guessed it—happens to be Kyoto's sister city. Consider this: You chat with a venerable Kyotoite who takes a swipe at what he calls the people out in the "country." As he spools forth with his yarn, you gradually decipher that the "country" he's referring to is Tokyo.

That's an overstatement. But Kyoto is the capital of culture, and they're rightfully proud of it. The long, narrow wooden townhouses and the lank streets that snake beside them exude a charm that Tokyo's concrete structures lack, however modern. The geisha of Gion help preserve the classical arts as they entertain their well-heeled guests with their dance, song and *shamisen* performances. Over in Nishijin, weavers and dyers, who've been handed down their expertise through the generations, painstakingly craft elegant silks.

But contemporary Kyoto is more than high-browed fashion; it's got high technology, too. Credit the potters of Kiyomizu for putting Kyoto's elegant ceramics on the map, but kudos to Kyocera for gobbling up the bulk of the world market with its ceramic packaging for semiconductors. In addition to *kabuki* and *no*, Kyoto originated the crafty Super Mario. Nintendo's young engineers keep developing newer generations of Japan's biggest cultural export: home videogames. But just a few blocks away from Nintendo's free-wheeling, Silicon Valley-like work environment, elderly women still toil at making tofu based on time-honored techniques.

34

35

36

34. The main hall of Kiyomizudera, a designated National Treasure, overlooks Kyoto. The temple's name means "pure water," and the water there is said to be a panacea.

35. The cobblestone paths of Kyoto's Ninenzaka will lead these Buddhist monks to the Yasaka Shrine, which attracts pilgrims and sightseers from all over Japan.

36. A storekeeper prepares *yakidofu*, lightly toasted bean curds high in protein. The split curtain, *noren*, indicates the shop is open for business.

37. A bevy of *maiko*, geisha apprentices, take time out to admire a newborn child and chat with the proud grandmother.

38. People sample the wares at the Kobo-no-ichi flea market on the grounds of the temple Toji in Kyoto.

37

38

Osaka and Nara: Of Business and Buddhism

"*Mokarimakka!*" the merchant woman says with a perky smile. Only in Osaka would "Did you make money?" substitute for "good morning." Although it's not used as often as it once was, the greeting mirrors the affably flamboyant merchant culture that continues to define Osaka. The swashbucklers of international finance—banks like Sanwa and Sumitomo—are headquartered here, as are consumer electronics titans, Matsushita Electric Industrial, Sanyo Electric, and Sharp.

Osakans are a passionate people with a knack for humor. The founder of McDonald's in Japan is a bona fide Osakan who's as good at managing the bottom line as he is at delivering the punch line. On why he targets they young: "800,000 Japanese die each year; 1.5 million are born. The 800,000

are scrapmetal. They won't eat burgers. But the 1.5 million will." Young or old, Osakans love their often hapless boys of summer, the Hanshin Tigers, the Chicago Cubs of Japan. "Even if they lose, they're cute," chimes an old fan.

Nearby Nara lacks the contemporary color of Osaka, for its greatness lies in its Buddhist past. In the eighth century, the country spent so much money building Japan's biggest bronze Buddha that it nearly went bankrupt. Its dedication at the temple Todaiji was one of the grandest events of the era, luring priests, musicians, and dancers from foreign lands such as Korea, China, and India. Likewise, 12 centuries later, international rock giants Bob Dylan and Joni Mitchell performed before the same Buddha at a UNESCO-sponsored concert there. Indeed, the big bronze and his bonzes are party animals at heart.

39. This sparkling new tower in Osaka affords a grand view of Osaka Castle. The area around the castle has sprouted into a new business center.

40. Shinsaibashi-suji is Osaka's largest shopping arcade.

41. You won't find Rudolph here, but the tame deer in Nara Park are just as friendly.

42. Nara's most prominent structure, the Daibutsuden (Great Buddha Hall) of Todaiji, keeps watch over the ancient city that once served as capital of Japan.

Japanese Industry: From Rice to Robots

Mention Japan, and most foreigners think of Toyotas and Sonys. Indeed, the engine that powered and propelled Japan's war-torn economy into a global juggernaut was industry. The diligence of Japan's work force, the long-term outlook of its managers, and support from a benevolent government helped produce the world's second largest economy after the United States. Matsushita Electric Industrial, a tiny electric socket maker in 1918, is today the world's largest consumer electronics conglomerate. And engineers at Japan's big automakers are also driven, turning out new models much faster than their European or American competitors.

A large part of the work force that oiled the machines and ran the assembly lines came from the countryside, and that meant a loss of farm labor. The muscle drain continues today, as young people shun farming and other jobs regarded as dirty, demanding, and dangerous. The aging agrarians left behind are shifting away from bulky vegetables to lighter items that are easier to harvest, like spinach and lettuce. Cultivators of rice, the spiritual symbol of Japanese agriculture, have long been shielded by the government from foreign competition. But they're in for tough times now that Japan has agreed to do what was once considered unthinkable: lift the lid on its rice market.

The old men of the sea also find it hard to lure young ones into the industry. What's more, the international adoption of fishery zones has sharply reduced Japan's open sea catch. To make up for that, Japan boosted its purchases from abroad and now ranks as the world's largest importer of marine products.

43. Japan boasts the world's biggest population of robots. These mechanical arms handle the welding chores at a Toyota plant in Aichi prefecture.

44. The day begins early for this vegetable vendor at an outdoor market in Akita Prefecture. Her produce comes fresh from the farm.

45. This extravaganza of colors comes from a sea of flags known as *tairyo-bata*. Fishermen fly them to thank the gods for their large catch and pray for fortune for the next sail.

46. Fishermen haul in their catch along the Pacific coast of Nantocho in Mie Prefecture.

47. Farm workers in Fukushima Prefecture plant rice seedlings the old way: by hand. Most farms now use machines to help out with this strenuous chore.

44

45

46

47

Japan's Village Consciousness: Better Together

The strong village mentality knits neighbors together in the countryside. If someone in the community needs to replace the thatched roof of his wooden farmhouse, the whole village of farmers turns up to lend a free hand.

And, of course, villagers congregate when it comes time for a festival. Fishermen and farmers toiling in the great outdoors depend on the good will of the gods for a bountiful harvest, so they participate out of the belief that the *kami* (deities) will help ward off natural disasters. In the dazzling Nebuta festival in Aomori, where floats carrying illuminated paper images of legendary characters are paraded through town, apple growers, rice farmers, and fishermen alike join together to cast the effigies out to sea on the final day in order to purify themselves.

Those fiestas, however, veil the problems plaguing the countryside. Walk through the main marketplace and the back roads, and you'll rarely encounter anyone in their 20s, for they have left for the urban excitement and snazzier employment opportunities of the cities. Their parents who tend the fields have trouble finding successors for the family business. And the young who don't leave the village have a taxing time finding women who are willing to marry into an agrarian household.

48. Villagers turn out to lend a hand to a neighbor who has to redo the thatched roof of his farmhouse in Shirakawa-go. Such favors help bind the village together.

49. The snow-covered A-frame farmhouses in Shirakawa-go lend the region an air of rusticity, just as log cabins do in the U.S.

50. Even Seurat's bathers didn't have it so good. Old-timers at this hot spring in Miyagi Prefecture forget their inhibitions and enjoy the communal spirit of unisex bathing, a once-common practice that went into decline with the advent of puritanical Western mores. Japanese hot springs profess to cure a variety of ailments, running the gamut from gall-bladder disease to gout.

51. Illuminated paper images atop floats light up the night in the Nebuta Festival. In the end, they're cast off to sea as part of a purification rite.

49

50

51

III

TRADITIONAL ARTS

Seeking the Eternal in the Ephemeral

by Martha J. McClintock

Like a cherry blossom that flourishes in brief splendor and then flutters away on a breeze, the lives, loves, and beauties of this world are all too fragile. The ephemeral, as embodied by the fleeting glory of flowers in bloom or the heroic final moments of a dying samurai warrior, is an ideal that has long been revered by the Japanese in their lives as well as in their art. Art in Japan, in all its manifestations, strives to capture, experience, and savor those heightened moments of aesthetic perfection in life—for a brief instant of beauty serves as an encapsulation of eternity. Even the short-lived splendor of a flower is a testament to the continuing rhythms of nature and the eternal cycle of its seasons.

The following pages will explore the variety of art in Japan, and reveal how the Japanese have, over the years, sought perfection in the beauty of the moment. The Japanese love of the ephemeral is epitomized by the temporary pause of a *kabuki* actor on stage or the accidental glaze drip on a ceramic jar. The eternal, on the other hand, is exemplified by the years of dedicated study and practice required to achieve these moments of perfection. The traditions of Japanese art are carefully handed down from master to disciple through the most rigorous of training programs. To cultivate the skills and grace of a professional geisha, the *maiko* apprentice must be trained from an early age in classical music and dance, as well as in all aspects of etiquette and behavior. Similarly, the lacquer artist, shrine carpenter, potter, and even *sumo* wrestler must engage in long years of preparation and training in order to excel in that given moment when they must perform their art.

The drama, excitement, and spiritual essence of Japan's arts are reflected in the lives of the Japanese, as many of these great artistic traditions have been incorporated into their daily routines. An elegantly coiffed secretary dons traditional clothing for her judo lesson, while a few hours a week practicing *no* chants lighten the load of an executive's busy schedule. Junior high school students stand in silent awe before a thousand year-old statue of Buddha, while nearby, a retired fisherman focuses his loving care on a small, ancient pine *bonsai*. And every spring, the evening newscaster gives a daily update on where the cherry trees have started to bloom in different areas of the country. Art, in all of its nuances, permeates contemporary life in Japan, as each fleeting encounter with beauty continues to inspire awe.

1. The Miyako Odori, a dance performed by geisha of the Gion district at the Kaburenjo Theater, Kyoto.

The Kabuki Spectacle

Begun as an open-air song and dance act in Kyoto during the early 17th century, *kabuki* has weathered scandals and evolved over the centuries to become Japan's liveliest traditional theater. Elaborate stage design, combined with the lavish costumes and makeup of the actors, heighten the dramatic tales of heroic samurai, villainous courtiers, and their long-suffering women.

Though it was originally performed by a young woman with a troupe of women players, *kabuki* is now the sole preserve of men. Actors belong to hereditary family guilds that specialize in a specific role or acting style, such as the female role known as *onnagata*, or the swaggering *aragoto* style used for male heroes or villains. *Kabuki* plays are divided into three main genres: *jidai-mono*, or historical plays with elaborate stage settings and large casts; *sewa-*

mono, or domestic plays portraying the lives of Edo-period (1600-1868) townspeople; and *shosagoto*, or dance-dramas focusing on dance performances and pantomime.

Current generations of the great acting families continue the *kabuki* tradition with a contemporary flair. Today, *kabuki* enjoys widespread popularity, with everyone from young office workers to grandmothers avidly following the latest news about their favorite actors.

2

2. Scene from *Sukeroku Yukari no Edo-zakura*, one of the "Eighteen Favorite Kabuki Plays." Courtesans display their finery in front of the Miura-ya brothel in the Yoshi-wara pleasure quarters.

3. The main character, Sukeroku, strikes a pose known as a *mie* as he struts down the *hanamichi*, the runway that extends out into the audience area. (Sukeroku played by Ichikawa Danjuro XII.)

4. Tadanobu fighting with Tota's men at the Fushimi Inari Shrine. Act II of the popular play, *Yoshitsune sembonzakura*. (Tadanobu played by Ichikawa Ennosuke III.)

3

4

No: Emotions Behind the Mask

A single pine tree painted on the back wall, and somber-robed musicians seated in front of it form the stark setting for the *no* stage. From the runway on the left, masked actors in lavish costumes slowly make their entrance onto the plain wooden stage to perform ancient plays—many of which are over 500 years old.

Originally the province of the aristocratic few, *no* is a theatrical form dating back to the 14th century that combines dance, chanting, and music. Actors and musicians perform their specified roles according to prescribed lyrics, movements, and staging. Like *kabuki*, *no* is traditionally performed only by men, although current generations of its hereditary troupes of actors and musicians teach their arts to a large number of female students as well.

Bunraku: Manipulation as Magic

Like *kabuki*, the *bunraku* puppet theater developed as an entertainment form for the urban classes of the Edo period (1600–1868). It combines puppetry with a style of chanting known as *joruri*, and musical accompaniment of the *shamisen*, a three-stringed instrument.

Unlike the puppets of the West, which are manipulated by strings, a *bunraku* puppet is handled directly by an onstage team of puppeteers who must endure years of training to show subtle movements and emotions in their meter-high dolls. The master puppeteer handles the head and right hand, while his black-hooded assistants move the other parts of the doll in carefully coordinated teamwork.

6

7

8

5. Matsukaze, the main character in this *no* play, dons the robe of her former lover Yukihira and performs a stylized dance. (From the play *Matsukaze*.)

6. *No* stage for the play *Matsukaze*. Two masked actors perform the roles of the sisters Matsukaze and Murasame. Musicians are seen seated at the back of the stage.

7. Master puppeteer, Yoshida Minosuke—a designated "National Living Treasure"—and his black-hooded assistants handle the puppet Omiwa in the "Golden Pavilion" scene in the *bunraku* play, *Imoseyama Onna Teikin*.

8. The puppet Ohatsu strikes a poignant pose in the final act of *The Love Suicides at Sonezaki*, as her lover, Tokubei, watches from behind. The main puppeteers are "National Living Treasures" Yoshida Bunjaku (Ohatsu) and Yoshida Tamao (Tokubei).

Martial Arts and Sumo: Grappling with the Mind

The martial arts in Japan are just that, martial and artistic. With philosophical underpinnings in *bushido*, "the way of the warrior," martial arts encourage the spiritual development of their practitioners. Lessons are often preceded by brief meditation sessions, and all matches begin and end with respectful bows. Today, the martial arts are practiced primarily on an amateur level, with frequent lessons and practice sessions leading on occasion to competitions. Like other traditional arts of Japan, they demand long years of training to perfect the requisite skills and attain the proper spiritual focus.

Though *sumo* technically is not a martial art, this ancient form of wrestling also requires rigorous mental and physical training. A popular spectator sport, *sumo* pits two wrestlers against each other in a brief shoving match that is lost if a wrestler falls, or steps outside the roped border of the sand ring.

Judo, which literally means "the way of softness," is a martial art that prizes agility and an acute mental assessment of the opponent over brute strength. Specific techniques allow even young female practitioners to level much larger opponents. Strikes, thrusts and kicks constitute the primary moves in karate. The characters for karate convey the meaning "empty hand," symbolizing the karate master's ability to best an opponent in unarmed combat. Karate was historically practiced in China and Okinawa. *Kendo*, the art of two-handed fencing with bamboo swords, is based on samurai sword techniques. It employs protective clothing and face masks which recall the armor worn by medieval warriors.

9

10

11

9. American-born Chad Rowan, who wrestles under the name of Akebono, is the current *yokozuna*, or grand champion. Here Akebono is seen with his two attendants in the ring entrance ritual, or *dohyo-iri*, that begins each day of the 15-day tournaments held six times a year.

10. Two *sumo* wrestlers grappling in a decisive moment as the referee looks on. The referee's ceremonial costume is modeled on the robes of an ancient courtier.

11. A single split-second move brings this judo contestant to the mat in this national martial arts tournament.

12. Sizing up one's opponent is an important skill in karate.

13. Two contestants in this *kendo* tournament parry thrusts with their bamboo swords.

12

13

Shinto Shrines and Buddhist Temples

The fundamental differences in the historical development of Shinto and Buddhism, the two main religions in Japan, are reflected in their contrasting architectural traditions. Shinto, a pantheistic, nature-based religion indigenous to Japan, places great emphasis on the concept of purity. It developed an architectural style characterized by plain, unvarnished wood, simple thatched or tile roofs, and gravel courtyards. The Ise Shrine serves as a testament to the simplicity of Shinto architecture. Dedicated to the Sun Goddess, the sacred inner compound of Ise can only be entered by shrine priests.

Buddhism, a religion that originated in India and developed on the Asian continent, was introduced to Japan in the 6th century from Korea, transmitting with it the traditions of Chinese and Korean art and architecture. Like their Christian counterparts, the Buddhist clergy in Japan spread the teachings and culture of their great religion from monasteries, which in Japan became thriving centers for Buddhist studies. One example is the temple complex of Horyuji, located just outside the city of Nara, whose central buildings date from the early 7th century and are recognized as the oldest wooden buildings in the world. The architectural methods and elements which can be seen preserved at Horyuji reflect Chinese temple architecture of the same period, most of which no longer remains on the Asian continent.

14

15

14. The central buildings of the Inner Shrine, part of the Ise Shrine complex. These buildings are rebuilt in exact replica every 20 years, employing ancient architectural forms, materials, and methods. The latest rebuilding occurred in 1993.

15. Aerial view of the western precinct of the temple Horyuji, located in the outskirts of Nara. The five-storied pagoda and the two-storied *kondo*, or golden hall, to its right are recognized as the oldest wooden buildings in the world.

16. A procession of Shinto priests enters the ceremonial rice field at the Ise Shrine to bless the first cuttings of the rice harvest.

16

Buddhist Sculpture: Myriad Faces

A small bronze statue of the Buddha was one of the artifacts brought into Japan during the 6th century by Korean envoys from Paekche who were credited with the introduction of Buddhism to Japan. During the centuries following this first importation of Buddhist images into the country, Japan developed its own sculptural traditions. The resulting body of Japanese sculpture represents a variety of gods and deities from the Buddhist pantheon, functioning either as central images of worship or as secondary, attendant figures.

The myriad faces of Buddhist sculpture range from serene images of the Amida Buddha and the goddess Kannon, to the fierce snarls of warriorlike guardian kings. Each Buddhist deity claims its own particular traits and attributes, symbolized in sculptural form by such physical details as the number of arms it has or the type of object it is holding. Succeeding generations of sculptors and individual sects of Buddhism developed their own expressive styles, creating lean, angular, and abstract figures, or fleshy and realistic forms.

Japanese temple settings are similarly diverse. Worship at small neighborhood or village temples may focus on one small central figure, while large temple complexes, like those built for the aristocracy in the Heian and Kamakura periods, include vast altar settings with more than a dozen sculptural forms. Whether observed in their original settings high upon the altars of Buddhist temples, or in the dim corridors of museum galleries, these fabulous figures of bronze or wood glow with inner dignity and power.

17

17. Shaka Triad, dated 623. Gilt bronze. Central figure, H. 86.4 cm. Horyuji temple, Nara. National Treasure.

18. Seated bodhisattva, Nyorin Kannon, 9th century. Polychrome wood. Figure, H. 109.4 cm. Kanshinji temple, Osaka. National Treasure.

19. Zochoten, one of the Four Guardian Kings, the Kaidando Hall of the temple Todaiji, Nara. Eighth century. Polychrome wood. H. 165.4 cm. National Treasure.

20. Amida Buddha and attendant figures on the central dais of the Golden Hall (Konjikido) of the temple Chusonji in Hiraizumi. Twelfth century. Central figure, H. 62 cm. National Treasure.

18

19

20

Painting and Woodblock Prints: Beauty in Diversity

Inspired by a rich religious and literary heritage, as well as a desire for the decorative and humorous, Japanese painters have over the centuries depicted almost every conceivable subject in a diverse range of styles. Much of Japanese religious and secular art has been greatly influenced by the painting traditions of China and Korea. Art forms with a strong continental flavor include Buddhist painting, which ranges from exquisitely detailed, polychrome images on silk to simple splashes of ink on paper.

Japanese secular art has also drawn its inspiration from Chinese and native literary traditions. The crowning glory of Japanese literature, *The Tale of Genji*—an 11th-century epic written by female courtier Murasaki Shikibu—has been reproduced in a number of lavish handscrolls, each recounting the story in beautiful calligraphy interspersed with illustrations.

Nature has been another major source of inspiration for Japan's painters and *ukiyo-e* woodblock printmakers. From Korin's brilliant design of dark green and royal blue irises across a pond of gold leaf, to Hokusai's humorous scene of a pair of men washing horses beneath a fabled waterfall, natural motifs enter into Japanese paintings and prints in a variety of forms.

Many *ukiyo-e* artists of the Edo period (1600–1868), like the mysterious Sharaku, depicted life in the pleasure quarters, taking as their subjects the world of *kabuki* and geisha. The affordable woodblock prints they produced, which served as the posters and advertisements of their day, are now treasured by art enthusiasts around the world.

21

22

23

21. *Fugen bosatsu.* 12th century, hanging scroll. Color and cut gold on silk. 159.0 × 74.5 cm. National Treasure. (Tokyo National Museum)

22. Section III of the Kashiwagi Chapter, *Tale of Genji Scrolls.* Twelfth century. Section of a handscroll painting, color on paper. 21.9 × 48.1 cm. National Treasure. (Tokugawa Art Museum, Nagoya)

23. *Irises* by Ogata Korin (1658–1716). Right screen of a pair of six-panel screens, color on gilded paper. Each screen, 150.9 × 338.8 cm. National Treasure. (Nezu Institute of Fine Arts, Tokyo)

24. *Ichikawa Ebizo as Takemura Sadanoshin* by Sharaku (act. 1794–95); oban (large format) woodblock print,

color and mica on paper. Important Cultural Property. (Tokyo National Museum)

25. *Yoshitsune Umaarai Waterfall of Yoshino, Washu Province*, from the series *Shokoku taki meguri* by Katsushika Hokusai (1760–1849). Oban (large format) woodblock print, color on paper. (Ota Memorial Museum of Art, Tokyo)

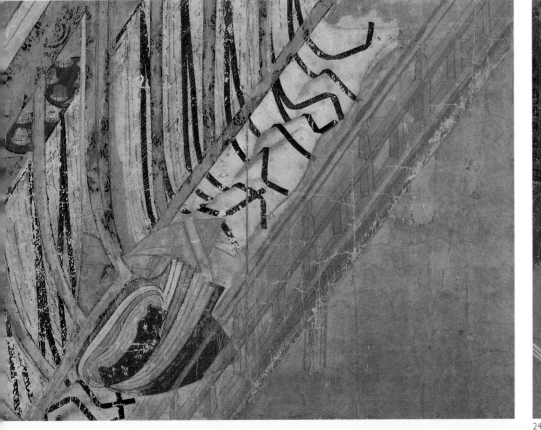

24

23

25

Castles and Palaces: The Samurai World of Power and Beauty

Feudal Japan was a nation of warring domains where castles defended clan territories by providing towers for look-outs and complicated labyrinths of corridors to confound intruders—while at the same time standing gracefully as visible symbols of the clan lords' power.

Himeji Castle, with its soaring tile roofs and glistening white walls, is beautiful testimony to the artistic sensibilities of castle architects and their patrons. The clever defense mechanisms built into the structure itself—the geometrically-shaped archers' loopholes placed at irregular intervals along the compound walls, or the trap windows from which a torrent of stones or hot oil could be unleashed upon would-be intruders—also attest to the supreme skill and ingenuity of the architects. In 1993 Himeji Castle was designated by UNESCO for protection as a world cultural heritage site.

Palaces, the urban mansions of clan lords, provided another symbol of their power. In grand residences like the Ninomaru Palace, located within the Nijo Castle compound in Kyoto, lavish paintings in gold and other brilliant colors covered the walls and ceilings of the main reception rooms. Here the lord would sit in state at the end of the room, while the select few admitted for his audience would be struck with awe at the dramatic setting before them. And here, the pine trees depicted on the walls surrounding them served as visual emblems of their lord's endurance and strength.

26

28

27

26. Himeji Castle, designated a National Treasure, rises in elegant splendor above a cloud of cherry trees. The central keep sits on a 45-meter hill. The five stories visible from the outside actually conceal seven internal stories.

27. Aerial view of the central keep of the Himeji Castle shows the labyrinth of walled passages which provides the final layer of protection against invasion. The tile roofs were impervious to flaming arrows, and the steep slope of the rock base wall thwarted those who tried to climb into the castle.

28. The Jodan-no-ma audience hall of the Ninomaru Palace, part of the Nijo Castle compound, Kyoto. The walls and coffered ceiling are decorated with paintings by the 17th-century artist, Kano Tanyu.

Zen Art

Zen, a school of Buddhism focused on individual meditation and personal enlightenment, developed in China and entered Japan in the Kamakura period (1185–1333). Zen monasteries became centers of learning and fostered such diverse arts as architecture, ink painting calligraphy, sculpture, and garden design. The ink painting traditions of China and Korea were introduced by Zen monks who traveled between Japan and the continent. The Japanese applications of these imported styles took the form of small album leaves such as Sesshu's *Winter Landscape*—which expresses the bright crackling air of winter in a single brush stroke down the center—or large nature scenes that spanned the walls of an abbot's quarters.

The spirit of meditation imbues many of Zen's art forms. Zen monks are trained to apply focusing techniques when writing even a single line of characters, which themselves often convey riddlelike Zen questions used during meditation sessions.

The unique garden form known as *karesansui*, or dry landscape, also is designed to inspire a mood of contemplation. Resembling the stark world of monochrome ink painting, these gardens of gravel, rock and evergreen bushes recreate mountainous landscapes in miniature. The careful weeding and raking of gravel required for these gardens are as much a part of the Zen monk's daily spiritual training as are his silent hours seated in the meditation hall.

29. Pair of hanging scrolls with calligraphy by Ikkyu Sojun (1394–1481), 48th abbot of the temple Daitokuji. Ink on paper. 133.5 × 41.5 cm. each. Important Cultural Properties. (Shinjuan, Daitokuji, Kyoto)

30. *Winter Landscape* by Sesshu Toyo (1420–1506). One of a pair of hanging scrolls. Ink on paper. 46.4 × 29.4 cm. National Treasure. (Tokyo National Museum)

31. Monks seated in meditation at the temple Sojiji in Yokohama.

32. *Karesansui* rock garden of the Daisen'in, a subtemple of the temple Daitokuji in Kyoto.

31

32

The Way of Tea: Refining the Rustic

Chanoyu, or the "way of tea," was developed in the 16th century by Sen no Rikyu, artistic advisor to the Shogun Toyotomi Hideyoshi. Based on the four principles of harmony, respect, purity, and tranquillity, the act of making and sharing a bowl of tea gave participants an aesthetic focus and peaceful respite from the war-torn strife of feudal Japan. Just as Marie Antoinette bid the creation of a village retreat where she could experience the "simple, carefree" life of the peasant, Hideyoshi and his successors commissioned tea masters like Rikyu to design gardens, villas, and tea ceremony rooms where they could savor an aura of rustic simplicity.

What looks like an old thatched-roof farmhouse, approached along a haphazard line of rocks leading across a stream, is actually the Shokintei, a tea pavilion set in the gardens of the famed Katsura Detached Palace. The display alcove in the tea room of the temple Myokian is constructed of rough, straw-filled plaster and weathered wood—specifications believed to have been given to temple carpenters by Rikyu himself.

The attempts to recreate the ideal of rustic simplicity continue today as thousands of students learn the tea ceremony, not only as training in traditional etiquette, but also to pursue the same goals of artistic and aesthetic tranquillity set out centuries ago by Rikyu.

33

33. Shokintei pavilion, Katsura Detached Palace, 17th century. Kyoto.

34. In this tea ceremony held in winter, the first guest drinks tea that has been made from hot water drawn from the kettle in the sunken hearth. The host is seated in the foreground.

35. Display alcove, or *tokonoma*, of the Taian, a tea house designed by Sen no Rikyu (1522–1591). The Taian is part of the Zen temple Myokian in Kyoto. Calligraphy scroll *Myoki* by Yamazaki Taiko, early 20th-century abbot of the temple Shokokuji in Kyoto.

34

35

Ikebana and Bonsai: Humanized Nature

Originating as floral offerings for Buddhist altar displays, *ikebana*, the art of Japanese flower arrangement, has developed over the centuries through a number of schools led by hereditary masters. Today, it is practiced by millions of students inside and outside Japan.

An *ikebana* arrangement is based on a precise number of flowers or branches, arranged in specific relationship to each other and to their container, with the particular formulas and techniques varying according to the school. The Ikenobo school, the oldest in Japan, has mastered the elegantly structured form of traditional *ikebana*, particularly in the *rikka* or standing flower arrangement style. Newer *ikebana* forms approach sculptural art in their size and complexity, often incorporating unusual materials such as paper

and wood. Set against the 17th-century wall paintings of the temple Nishi Honganji in Kyoto, this massive arrangement (*no. 36, below*) by Teshigahara Hiroshi, current head of the Sogetsu school of *ikebana*, is a perfect blend of the contemporary and the traditional.

Specific techniques and rigorous care are required to cultivate the dwarf trees and plants known as *bonsai*. Literally "tray plants," *bonsai* are kept in shallow planters and must be constantly trimmed and repotted in order to maintain their stunted appearance. Successfully nurtured *bonsai* can live for more than a hundred years. The pine tree, a traditional Japanese symbol of eternity, is especially popular among *bonsai* artists, who must devote many years of their lives toward the meticulous care of their trees.

36

37

38

Ceramics and Lacquerware: Elegance for the Wealthy Few

While Japanese ceramics and lacquerware have been created in immeasurable diversity, they can be roughly classified by the contrasting aesthetics they represent. A plain black Raku ware tea bowl epitomizes the austere simplicity preferred by practitioners of the Japanese tea ceremony, just as a lacquered wooden box, weathered by constant use, characterizes the utilitarian emphasis of *mingei*, or folk crafts. The gorgeous, richly decorated ceramics and lacquerware on these pages espouse a very different aesthetic reflecting the sumptuous tastes of the wealthy and privileged.

Ornamental ceramics and lacquerware were originally created for the aristocratic class, based on models imported from China. The changing times of the Edo period led to the wider dispersal of personal wealth, giving rise to a prosperous merchant class which, along with the old samurai elite, became the principal patrons for these ornate, highly decorative wares. Paralleling this growing demand for the opulent was the creation of uniquely Japanese motifs and shapes that differed from those of the imported wares from China.

The Kakiemon family in Kyushu developed a distinctive form of colorful, finely decorated overglaze enamel porcelains, while Nabeshima clan lords isolated their potters from outside contact to protect the secrets of their translucent overglaze porcelains. Elegant *maki-e* lacquerware embellished with powdered gold was used for all types of personal equipment such as cosmetic boxes, bowls, and dishes. *Maki-e* techniques can also be found in document cases and reading stands used for Buddhist sutras or theatrical texts.

39

40

39. In the Kakiemon tradition, flowers and other motifs are painted in overglaze enamel on porcelain that has initially been fired with only a clear glaze. Once the piece has been painted with overglaze enamels, it is then refired to bring out the true brilliance of the colors.

40. Set of five small dishes, Nabeshima ware. Design of palm fronds in overglaze enamels. Edo period, 17th-18th century. Each dish, H. 4.5 cm., mouth D. 14.8 cm., bottom D. 8.1 cm. (MOA Museum of Art, Shizuoka)

41. Inlaid lacquer box *Yatsuhashi* by Ogata Korin (1658–1716). Black lacquer inlaid with gold, mother of pearl, and lead. L. 27.4 x W. 19.7 x H. 14.2 cm. National Treasure. (Tokyo National Museum)

42. Tea-leaf storage jar by Nonomura Ninsei (fl. mid. 17th century). Glazed stoneware, H. 36 cm. (Fukuoka Museum of Art, Fukuoka)

43. Reading stand with design of autumn flowers and paulownia crests. Overall H. 57.0 cm., face of reading surface, L. 29.2 x W 37.5 cm. (Tokyo National Museum)

41

42

43

Mingei: The Utilitarian Beauty of Folk Crafts

First coined by Yanagi Muneyoshi in 1926, the term *mingei*, or folk crafts, came to symbolize a diverse movement to recognize and appreciate the beauty of utilitarian objects made by unknown artisans. It refers to a whole wealth of handcrafted objects comprising metalwork, textiles, ceramics, furniture, and bamboo ware.

Each region in Japan's mountainous archipelago developed crafts that suited the practical needs of the community and reflected local tastes and traditions. The *mingei* movement strove not only to locate and catalog these wares, but also to ensure the future survival of handicraft industries, which were threatened by an onslaught of mass-produced, machine-manufactured goods. Bernard Leach (1887–1979), an English potter and author, worked

with the founders of the *mingei* movement to link their efforts with folk art movements in Britain and Europe.

The taste for these handmade objects persists today against the encroaching modernization and mechanization of even the remotest corners of Japan. The unassuming elegance characterizing the *mingei* aesthetic has also been recognized by collectors outside the country, and today, handcrafted items such as stoneware jars, Okinawan textiles, and wooden *tansu* cabinets can be found in the U.S., Europe, South America, and other areas around the world.

44

45

46

44. Stoking the fire through a hole in the side wall of a *noborigama*, or climbing kiln, in the pottery village of Mashiko in Tochigi Prefecture.

45. Large bowl by Hamada Shoji. Stoneware, iron glaze dripped over white ground. 1963. D. 58 cm. (Japan Folk Crafts Museum, Tokyo)

46. Large storage jar. Tamba stoneware, natural ash glaze. Muromachi period (1333–1568). H. 41.5 cm. (Japan Folk Crafts Museum, Tokyo)

47. Ceremonial hood garment (*kazuki*). Indigo-dyed hemp with resist designs. Eighteenth century. 151 × 132.5 cm. (Japan Folk Crafts Museum, Tokyo)

48. Okinawan *bingata* kimono. Cotton with stenciled designs of plants and birds. Nineteenth century. 130 × 113 cm. (Japan Folk Crafts Museum, Tokyo)

49. Sea chest (*funa-dansu*). Wood with iron fittings. Eighteenth century. H. 47.5 × W. 42 × D. 51 cm. *Funa-dansu* were used aboard large trading ships as safes for money and important documents. (Japan Folk Crafts Museum, Tokyo)

47

48

49

Beyond Paradigm:
Art as Life in Contemporary Japan

by Azby Brown

Culture is like a soup. Wherever one goes on the planet, one encounters blends of color and flavor, of carefully nurtured ideas mingling with the blunt and rough-cut. In this sense, the culture of contemporary Japan presents one of the most engrossing mixtures of indigenous and foreign, traditional and newly developed arts in the world. And this "state-of-the-arts" is also a reflection of the lives of the people themselves.

When one thinks of contemporary Japan, Tokyo instantly presents itself as characteristic. A compendium of architectural languages and found imagery so dense, so chaotic, so unexpected in its brilliance and ability to appall, Tokyo defies all prior yardsticks of the "natural" and the "cultured." Yet hidden underneath is a great and beautiful sense pleading to be brought to light: a tremendous amount of local color and neighborhood ways.

But Tokyo is not all of Japan. History has conspired to give the country a bipolar configuration, with the authority of Tokyo balanced by the combined weight of Kyoto and Osaka, the two major cities of the Kansai region. While Osaka dominates the economic and political life of this region, Kyoto maintains its claim to cultural sophistication. And where contemporary arts are concerned, their sensibilities are indeed distinct. The arts in outlying prefectures tend to be supported by single institutions or patrons; confronted with the vibrancy of the "art worlds" in Tokyo, Kyoto and Osaka, it is difficult for the practitioners in these more remote areas to resist the call of the metropolis.

The understrata of Japanese cities are composed of natural topography and human history. Physical restrictions and the necessities of defense divided Osaka and Tokyo into mazelike warrens of gated communities with distinct identities, all linked by narrow streets. Kyoto was easier to overrun because of its gridlike configuration originally laid out some 2,000 years ago. "Castle towns" like Kanazawa still maintain a concentric structure, while others like Takayama mimic Kyoto's grid.

Today, life in most of these cities is confined by a lack of space—a condition dealt by the overwhelmingly mountainous topography of the islands. That present designers have been able to make this constraint itself seem like a comfortable virtue is one of the great cultural inheritances contemporary Japan will bequeath to the future world. The influence of this "miniaturizing" aesthetic—which emphasizes beauty on a compact, human scale—has already been felt in the West for over 100 years.

Recently, Japan's contemporary architecture, fashion, and design have achieved world recognition, and it seems likely that Japanese methods and sensibilities will continue to inspire the West. For Japan, in all its contrasting splendor, is a chaotic, ongoing work of art-as-life that compels you to watch, and to participate.

1. The "Flamme d'or" crowning Philippe Starck's Asahi Beer Azumabashi Hall gestures as if issuing a challenge to the traditional neighborhood of Asakusa across the Sumida River in Tokyo.

Tokyo: Showcase of Modernization

Tokyo was forced to abandon its former name, Edo, when it was designated the new capital of Japan in 1868. As the national showcase of modernization, Tokyo became the site of the most visible architectural and cultural experimentation. With its factories and offices attracting millions of workers and bureaucrats from the far-flung provinces, it became, if you will, the "America" of Japan—a new society, progressive and driven, composed primarily of immigrants wanting the quintessential urban experience. Today, only one in four Tokyoites was actually born there, and even fewer families have called Tokyo home for two or more generations.

If the cultural project of Tokyo has been to gather the best the nation has to offer and present it to the outside world, that it is an amalgam with no single style should go without saying. And yet Tokyo is marked by degree, by extremity: the biggest buildings, the most expensive restaurants, the newest dance music.

If there is a style, it comes from the social status and wealth of its patrons. It is generally more experimental, as Tokyo's inhabitants are better traveled and consequently more acutely aware of overseas trends. In this sense internationalism is pursued with great enthusiasm, though the results may often seem humorous.

2

2–5. Tokyo's compulsive rush to remake itself provides the perfect palate for eager architects, and many were given free reign on Rinkai Fukutoshin—a stretch of reclaimed land in Tokyo Bay: a view of the new island, with the Ariake Sports Center 's signature dome in the upper left corner and central Tokyo in the background (*left*); one of several outdoor sculptures fronting Tokyo Big Sight, the new exhibition complex (*top right*); the Fuji Television Building and a state-of-the-art driverless monorail (*middle*); and the Rainbow Bridge, Tokyo's multicolored illuminated span (*bottom right*).

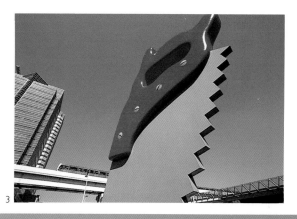

3

4

5

Kansai: Kyoto and Osaka's Vigorous Synthesis

If the contemporary arts of Tokyo are focused outward—to the international scene, to global recognition—and sometimes seem to have jettisoned traditional culture in order to become more accessible abroad, much recent art from Kyoto reflects a healthy synthesis between new and old.

Despite the rampages of real estate development, this ancient capital has managed to maintain its original élan and esprit. Recent Kyoto pottery and lacquerware, for instance, apply time-honored techniques to items of contemporary outline, allowing the materials to shine through. Architecture in the city has long been faced with the need to generate exquisitely detailed and fashionable entertainment spaces along tile-roofed back streets. There is more renovation in Kyoto than in either Tokyo or Osaka, and it is usually bet-ter done, the best exhibiting both sensitivity to tradition as well as a sense of adventure.

But of the three major cities, Osaka remains the most exuberant. While less pretentious than Tokyo, a little scratching reveals a "second city" complex that compels its inhabitants onward to even greater and faster achievements than those of the capital. In the visual arts, many Osakaites have achieved international standing without having to leave their chaotic neighborhoods, an almost unheard-of occurrence prior to the late 1980s. If Tokyo arts show a face that desires to be accepted abroad, and Kyoto arts point the way to a harmonious future, Osaka tells it like it is. Recent architecture in Osaka aims first and foremost to be unforgettable. And it often is.

6

7

6. In a city nurturing twelve centuries of tradition, the unabashedly modern Kyoto Station Building hardly bolsters the image of the ancient capital, but its decidedly upscale vibrancy has drawn youthful crowds from every corner of Japan.

7. The most striking new monument on the Osaka skyline is this Umeda Sky Building by Hara Hiroshi.

8. In Kyoto, one may come across tasteful but stimulating renovations of traditional buildings such as the office of architect Wakabayashi Hiroyuki, whose demure exterior conceals…

9. …a somewhat more updated interior.

9

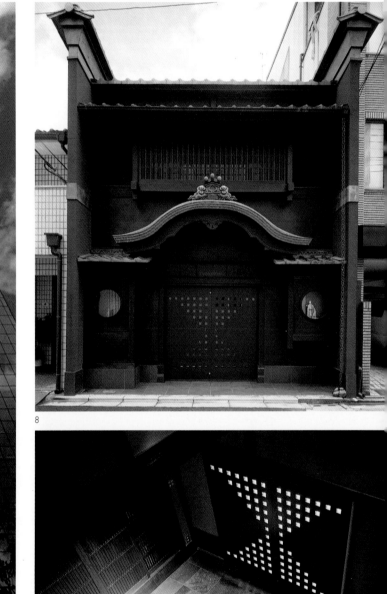

8

Outside the Metropolis

Partly as a result of boom-decade government policy, even mid-sized cities now boast new museums which regularly display contemporary art from home and abroad as well as historical stand-bys. Complexes such as Mito's Art Tower feature concert halls and theaters as well. But the best new theater and dance are usually found at some of the dozens of small spaces scattered throughout the major cities, particularly in areas frequented by the young.

Many arts festivals are held in relatively unspoilt rural areas, where one can see performances and artworks by leading world cultural figures. These include performances of contemporary theater at Toga-mura, and avant-garde and traditional dance, music, and visual art at Hakushu-mura in Yamanashi Prefecture. While organizers like Hakushu's Tanaka Min live and maintain their studios at these locations, participants are drawn from all over, and are often city-dwellers longing for a change of routine and a natural stimulus. The relaxed and picnic-like atmosphere allows both performers and audience to be more receptive to experimentation and impromptu collaboration. And of course, these experiences nourish and reinvigorate the urban arts themselves.

10. Performances at the Toga International Arts Festival take place on the open-air stage designed by architect Isozaki Arata.

11. The Hakushu Summer Art Festival happens amidst rice fields and a chicken farm. Many sculptors, such as Haraguchi Noriyuki, contribute works like this water-filled stage which double as performance sites.

10

11

JAPAN: FACTS AND FIGURES

CAPITAL:	Tokyo
LANGUAGE:	Japanese
POPULATION (1991)[1]:	124,043,000
MONETARY UNIT:	Yen
MAJOR RELIGIONS:	Buddhism, Shintoism
HEAD OF GOVERNMENT:	Prime Minister
SYMBOL OF STATE:	Emperor

LAND

Japan consists of an archipelago extending roughly 300 kilometers from northeast to southwest. It lies in the temperate monsoon zone of East Asia. The climate varies widely from north to south, with the northern island of Hokkaido occupying the sub-arctic zone, and the southern islands of Okinawa located in the subtropic zone.

- Total Land Area[2]:
  377,737 km²

- Area of Main Islands[3]:

Honshu	231,123 km²
Hokkaido	83,408 km²
Kyushu	44,410 km²
Shikoku	18,796 km²

- Highest Elevation[4]:
  Mt. Fuji—3,776 meters

- Administrative Divisions:
  43 prefectures, 2 *fu* (urban prefectures), 1 *do* and metropolitan Tokyo

PEOPLE/LIFE

With a population of 124 million, Japan boasts a large, affluent, and well-educated society. Japanese citizens enjoy the longest average life expectancy and one of the highest per capita incomes in the world. Yet the quality of life, especially in urban areas, is constrained by high prices and cramped housing conditions. In the coming decades, much attention will focus on Japan's growing number of elderly citizens—by the year 2020, the Ministry of Health and Welfare predicts that one out of every four Japanese will be 65 and over, which would give Japan the largest elderly population in the world.

- Per Capita GDP (1993)[5]:
  $34,910

- Average Life Expectancy (1994)[6]:
  Male—76.25 years
  Female—82.51 years

- Average Working Hours/Year, Manufacturing Industry (1993)[7]:
  Japan—2,017 hours
  U.S.—1,957 hours

SOURCES:
1 Management and Coordination Agency.
2 Geographical Survey Institute.
3 Geographical Survey Institute.
4 Geographical Survey Institute.
5 Economic Planning Agency.
6 Ministry of Health and Welfare.
7 Ministry of Labor.
8 Bank of Japan.